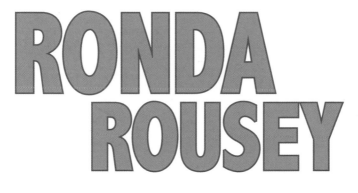

RONDA ROUSEY

Written by Steve Pantaleo

Reader

Penguin
Random
House

Project Editor Pamela Afram
Designer Elena Jarmoskaite
Senior Designer Lisa Robb
Senior Pre-Production Producer Marc Staples
Producer Louise Daly
Managing Editor Paula Regan
Managing Art Editor Jo Connor
Art Director Lisa Lanzarini
Publisher Julie Ferris
Publishing Director Simon Beecroft

Reading Consultant Linda B. Gambrell, PhD

First American Edition, 2020
Published in the United States by DK Publishing
1450 Broadway, Suite 801, New York, NY 10018

Page design copyright ©2020 Dorling Kindersley Limited
DK, a Division of Penguin Random House LLC
20 21 22 23 24 10 9 8 7 6 5 4 3 2 1
001–316350–Jan/2020

A catalog record for this book is available from the Library of Congress.
ISBN 978-1-4654-8993-7 (Paperback)
ISBN 978-1-4654-9056-8 (Hardback)

DK books are available at special discounts when purchased in bulk for sales
promotions, premiums, fund-raising, or educational use. For details, contact:
DK Publishing Special Markets, 1450 Broadway, Suite 801, New York, NY 10018
SpecialSales@dk.com

Printed and bound in China

A WORLD OF IDEAS:
SEE ALL THERE IS TO KNOW

www.dk.com
www.wwe.com

Contents

Meet Ronda Rousey

Ronda Rousey is a mixed martial arts (MMA) fighter. She has battled some of the toughest women in the world.

Now Ronda is a WWE Superstar! She is ready to take on the best female Superstars in the ring.

"Rowdy" Roddy Piper

When she was a girl, Ronda's hero was the Superstar Roddy Piper. She wanted to be just like him. Piper gave Ronda his nickname, "Rowdy." Ronda wears ring gear just like Roddy's.

Roddy Piper holds Ric Flair above his head.

Getting ring ready

Ronda always dreamed of being a WWE Superstar. She began training at the WWE Performance Center. Superstars and coaches helped her get ready for the ring.

Ronda stretches her muscles.

Ronda training with WWE Superstar Kurt Angle.

Rowdy in the ring

Ronda went to see *WrestleMania 31*.
The Rock saw her in the crowd. He
invited her into the ring. The crowd
was delighted.

However, WWE bosses Stephanie McMahon and Triple H did not like Ronda. They wanted Ronda out of the ring!

From MMA to WWE

Ronda's MMA moves help her in the ring. Her judo throws show skill and strength.

Ronda's submission hold is called an Arm Bar. Ronda grips tightly on to Dana Brooke's arm. Dana has no choice but to tap out!

MMA fighters in WWE

Ronda is not the only MMA fighter to join WWE. These Superstars have also proven their skills in WWE.

NAME: Shayna Baszler

HEIGHT: 5ft 7in

SIGNATURE MOVE:
Kirifuda Clutch

NICKNAME:
"The Queen of Spades"

NAME: Bobby Lashley

HEIGHT: 6ft 3in

WEIGHT: 273lb

SIGNATURE MOVE:
The Dominator

NICKNAME:
"The Almighty"

NAME:

Brock Lesnar

HEIGHT: 6ft 3in

WEIGHT: 286lb

SIGNATURE MOVE:

F-5

NICKNAME:

"The Beast"

NAME:

Ken Shamrock

HEIGHT: 6ft 1in

WEIGHT: 243lb

SIGNATURE MOVE:

Ankle Lock

NICKNAME:

"The World's Most Dangerous Man"

Keeping control

Triple H and Stephanie McMahon want to keep Ronda under their control. Ronda does not want to be controlled by anyone.

When Ronda learns of their plans, she lets Triple H and Stephanie know who is in charge!

Mixed Tag Team Match

Ronda teams up with Kurt Angle.
They battle Stephanie McMahon
and Triple H at *WrestleMania 34*
in a Mixed Tag Team Match.

It is Ronda's first WWE match. The crowd is amazed at her skill in the ring. Ronda and Angle have won!

Ronda's strength

Training for matches has given Ronda incredible strength. She can lift Superstars onto her shoulders. She can slam them down onto the mat.

Ronda carries Triple H on her shoulders at *WrestleMania 34*.

Ronda does not care whether she is facing a male or a female Superstar. She will battle anyone who stands in her way!

The Real Horsewomen

Some of Ronda's MMA friends create a faction called the Four Horsewomen. They follow Ronda to WWE.

Ronda's Horsewomen

WWE already has its own team with the same name! One day, the two teams will battle.

WWE's Horsewomen

Ronda vs. Stephanie

Stephanie McMahon likes to boss people around. This makes Ronda angry. Ronda and Stephanie battle in the ring. Ronda uses her Arm Bar move on Stephanie. It hurts! Stephanie gives up.

Many achievements

Ronda joined WWE in 2018. Since then, she has impressed the WWE Universe with her many achievements.

231-DAY CHAMP!

Ronda held the *RAW* Women's Championship for 231 days. That is the longest ever reign!

UNDEFEATED!

Ronda went undefeated by any WWE Superstar for a full year.

MAIN EVENT STAR!

Ronda earned the right to headline *WrestleMania 35*.

Battling Nia Jax

Nia Jax picks Ronda to be her challenger for the *RAW* Women's Championship. Nia is bigger and stronger, but Ronda isn't afraid.

Ronda battles Nia at *Money in the Bank*. Ronda leaps off the ropes to knock Jax down. Ronda nearly wins, but Nia's friend, Alexa Bliss, saves Nia!

Becoming RAW Women's Champion

Ronda wants revenge against Alexa Bliss. Alexa ruined Ronda's chances against Nia Jax. A match is set at *SummerSlam*. Ronda locks Bliss in a painful Arm Bar hold. Ronda wins the match and becomes *RAW* Women's Champion!

Women in WWE

These women are all in the WWE Hall of Fame. They inspired today's female Superstars, including Ronda.

TRISH STRATUS

Trish won seven Women's Championships. She was an amazing athlete.

CHYNA

Chyna was so powerful, she was nicknamed "The Ninth Wonder of the World."

JACQUELINE

This champion was really tough. She also helped train Superstars.

BETH PHOENIX

Nicknamed "The Glamazon," Beth was flashy and strong.

LITA

This daring Superstar loved to flip through the air. She was often called "extreme."

Undefeated champion

Ronda wins 11 matches for the *RAW* Women's Championship. This makes her the undefeated champion. A true champion will defend their title. Ronda won't let her title go without a fight!

Ronda sets up Nikki Bella for an Arm Bar.

Ronda tosses Sasha Banks with a Piper's Pit move.

Ronda traps
Ruby Riott in
an Arm Bar.

Ronda's revenge

SmackDown Superstars invade *RAW*! Becky Lynch is the brash *SmackDown* Women's Champion. She argues with Ronda backstage!

Weeks later, Ronda gets revenge in the ring. She pushes Becky and Charlotte Flair off a giant ladder!

Challenge accepted

Becky Lynch wins the 2019 Women's Royal Rumble Match. She challenges Ronda to a match at *WrestleMania*.

Charlotte Flair is added to
the match. The three Superstars
brawl in the ring.

Finding an ally

Natalya helped Ronda train to be a Superstar. Now they are friends and tag team partners.

Ronda and Natalya work
together to win matches. It is
hard for their rivals to beat them
when they work together.

The main event

WWE holds the first women's main event in history at *WrestleMania 35*! Ronda takes on two other female Superstars in a tough battle.

Ronda loses the match and the *RAW* Women's Championship, but she proves herself in the ring. It won't be long before she is a champion once again!

Quiz

1. Where did Ronda get her nickname, "Rowdy"?

2. Which Superstar asked Ronda to join him in the ring at *WrestleMania 31*?

3. True or false: Ronda held the *RAW* Women's Championship for 250 days.

4. Which Superstar saves Nia Jax in her *Money in the Bank* match?

5. What is Beth Phoenix's nickname?

6. True or false: Ronda's submission hold is called an Arm Bar.

7. Who does Ronda push off a giant ladder?

8. What is the name of Ronda's faction?

9. How many Superstars did Ronda battle in the main event at *WrestleMania 35*?

10. Who is Ronda's ally?

Answers on page 46

Glossary

achievement
Something a person has done very well.

brash
Rude and loud.

faction
A group of Superstars.

revenge
When a person gets back at someone who did something wrong to them.

undefeated
Having never lost a match.

Answers to the quiz on pages 44 and 45:
1. From "Rowdy" Roddy Piper 2. The Rock 3. False; she held it for 231 days 4. Alexa Bliss 5. "The Glamazon"
6. True 7. Becky and Charlotte 8. The Four Horsewomen
9. Two 10. Natalya

Index

A LEVEL FOR EVERY READER

This book is a part of an exciting four-level reading series to support children in developing the habit of reading widely for both pleasure and information. Each book is designed to develop a child's reading skills, fluency, grammar awareness, and comprehension in order to build confidence and enjoyment when reading.

Ready for a Level 2 (Beginning to Read) book
A child should:
- be able to recognize a bank of common words quickly and be able to blend sounds together to make some words.
- be familiar with using beginner letter sounds and context clues to figure out unfamiliar words.
- sometimes correct his/her reading if it doesn't look right or make sense.
- be aware of the need for a slight pause at commas and a longer one at periods.

A valuable and shared reading experience
For many children, reading requires much effort, but adult participation can make reading both fun and easier. Here are a few tips on how to use this book with a young reader:

Check out the contents together:
- read about the book on the back cover and talk about the contents page to help heighten interest and expectation.
- discuss new or difficult words.
- chat about labels, annotations, and pictures.

Support the reader:
- give the book to the young reader to turn the pages.
- where necessary, encourage longer words to be broken into syllables, sound out each one, and then flow the syllables together; ask him/her to reread the sentence to check the meaning.
- encourage the reader to vary her/his voice as she/he reads; demonstrate how to do this if helpful.

Talk at the end of each book, or after every few pages:
- ask questions about the text and the meaning of the words used—this helps develop comprehension skills.
- read the quiz at the end of the book and encourage the reader to answer the questions, if necessary, by turning back to the relevant pages to find the answers.

Series consultant, Dr. Linda Gambrell, Distinguished Professor of Education at Clemson University, has served as President of the National Reading Conference, the College Reading Association, and the International Reading Association.